A Master Class with Warren Buffett and Charlie Munger 2014

The Q&A Sessions of the 2014 Berkshire Hathaway Inc. Shareholders Meeting

by

Eben Otuteye, PhD
and
Mohammad Siddiquee, MBA

Copyright © 2015 Otuteye and Siddiquee

All rights reserved. No part of this book may be used or reproduced, stored in a retrieval system, or transmitted in any form or by any means, electronic, mechanical or otherwise without prior written permission from the publisher.

Cover Design: Chris Houliez

ISBN 13: 978-1505847215
ISBN 10: 1505847214

Disclaimer: This book is for educational purposes only. These notes are not verified or approved by Warren Buffett, Charlie Munger, nor by any director or officer of Berkshire Hathaway Inc. We relied primarily on our handwritten notes from the meeting and cross-checked them with other people's notes. This publication is not meant to offer investment advice. No part of the information in this book should be considered a recommendation to purchase or sell any security.

Eppley Airfield, Omaha, Photo: Mohammad Siddiquee

Table of Contents

Preface 7

Preliminaries 13

Questions and Answers: Part 1 19

Questions and Answers: Part 2 55

Epilogue 93

About the Authors 95

Index..99

Preface

Every generation has its legends. For this generation and in the domain of investments, Warren Buffett and his longtime partner, Charlie Munger, are definitely investment legends of our time. Between them, they have over 120 years of combined experience in investment, not counting the fact that Warren Buffett bought his first stock when he was eleven years old (six shares of Cities Services, now known as CITGO, an oil company). What makes them legends is not just the number of years of experience in active investment but also the wisdom of their modus operandi as testified to by the consistent and outstanding results delivered for over sixty years. If common sense and logic ruled the investment world, everyone should be investing like Warren Buffett and Charlie Munger.

We would be remiss to talk about Warren Buffett's investment prowess without acknowledging Benjamin Graham, the "Dean of Wall Street", and father of value investing. Warren always acknowledges Ben Graham as the one who had the most influence on him as an investor. Warren Buffett was Benjamin Graham's student, then became Ben Graham's employee and a lifetime family friend. Warren carefully studied and followed the principles and philosophies of Graham for years. And it only got better when he met Charlie Munger and the two of them perfected their system of investment and business portfolio management.

There is no question that if you practice what they teach and practice themselves, you cannot help but be successful in investment. Sadly, most of Wall Street and academia doesn't get this. Apart from their investment and management skills, Buffett and Munger are also great teachers. They know how to make their points so clearly and succinctly that everyone can understand. They also know how to express them in a way that you will never forget, especially when there's a bit of a sting in it, as is the case sometimes from Charlie. That is what the reader will find by reading these questions and answers from the May 2014 Berkshire Annual General Meeting (AGM).

The AGM of the shareholders of Berkshire Hathaway Inc., dubbed the "Woodstock for Capitalists," is nothing like the typical run-of-the-mill meeting of shareholders to elect directors and discuss the fiscal state of a company. Apart from the fun and fanfare, it is a great opportunity to tap into the wisdom storehouse of Warren Buffett and Charlie Munger in finance, investment, business management, and economics—and even life in general.

Being relatively new to Berkshire AGM, we thought we could prepare ourselves by reading some material on it. Apart from reading Warren Buffett's letters to shareholders and the Berkshire annual reports, the main resource we consulted was the book *Pilgrimage to Warren Buffett's Omaha* by Jeff Mathews. In the process we realized that there's no reliable and readily available source to access the Q&A sessions of past AGMs. It is our opinion that majority of those who attend the meeting are keen and teachable learners who will appreciate a reference source to review the questions and answers of the meeting. Hence, the motivation for this book. We hope both Warren Buffett and Charlie Munger will stick around for a while and maintain this format of the annual meeting in order to give us the opportunity to continue to tap into their wisdom. For that reason we also hope to make this book the first of an annual series.

Another motivation for the book is that both of us came to know about Warren Buffett and Charlie Munger rather late (Eben in early 2000s and Mohammad in 2010). The reason is that although we spent a lot of time in business schools, none of our instructors introduced us to them (or to Ben Graham). That is one regret we share—the lost opportunity of not knowing Warren Buffett and Charlie Munger earlier in life. We figured the way to make up for this, now that we're instructors, is to introduce our students very early in their business school education to the ideas of these legendary investors. Writing this series is our way of contributing to the efforts of those who are committed to spreading the word about the right way to invest, to think about money, and to manage a business, as exemplified by Warren Buffett and Charlie Munger. This is the first in a series of publications by which we intend to disseminate the ideas of Warren Buffett and Charlie Munger. We believe that will be a great service to society.

About the Title of the Book

On May 6, 2014, Bill Gates posted a blog[1] that began:

> "In the arts, a master class is a group lesson with an acknowledged expert—a chance for students to hear from an undisputed master and to improve their work by being exposed to the best.
>
> This last weekend, I joined almost forty thousand other 'students' to attend the master class for investors that is the Berkshire Hathaway annual meeting."

That blog resonated immediately with us and we decided to use the title of the blog as the title of this book. The Berkshire Hathaway AGM is indeed a master class with legends.

Accuracy of Content

As those who attend the AGM are aware, part of the protocol is that no electronic recording equipment is permitted. Thus everything you read here was first written down. Although we tried to transcribe what was said as accurately as possible, we weren't able to make a verbatim copy. A number of expressions are paraphrases of what was actually said. However,

---

[1] http://www.gatesnotes.com/About-Bill-Gates/Master-Class-with-Warren-Buffett-Berkshire-Hathaway-Annual-Meeting-2014

we've made every effort to preserve the sense and meaning of what was said. We also consulted a number of websites to cross-check our notes. While our words are not always identical to others', we're satisfied that the content is an accurate representation of what was said. Of course, the punctuation is entirely our creation.

Berkshire Hathaway 2014 Annual Shareholders' Meeting Notes

Saturday, May 3, 2014
CenturyLink Center
455 North 10th Street, Omaha NE 68102

Preliminaries

Opening Remarks

The meeting started with a video entertainment. A one-hour humorous animated film of a future Winter Olympics hockey gold-medal showdown between the U.S. and Russia is taking place in Omaha. The U.S. team is led by Warren Buffett, Charlie Munger, and Bill Gates. Russia's muscular players threaten to beat the relatively diminutive American team "into borscht." With the score tied late, coach Ajit Jain [manages Berkshire Hathaway Reinsurance Group] calls a time-out and designs a trick play. He holds up a small whiteboard containing several complex mathematical equations and states that this play has "an 87% chance of success." When play is resumed, a desk from Nebraska Furniture Mart appears on the ice, moving in the direction of the Russian goal. Charlie Munger, who was moving the desk forward and hiding behind it, suddenly appears and shoots the puck into the net. The U.S. wins 4-3.

The video also humorously depicted Warren Buffett and Paul Anka [a Canadian singer, songwriter and actor] singing a rendition of "My Way"— originally made famous by Frank Sinatra [an American singer, actor, director, and producer] and written by Paul Anka.

Q&A Format

The format of the Q&A session was similar to the last five annual meetings. Three business journalists—Andrew Ross Sorkin, CNBC and *New York Times;* Becky Quick, CNBC; and Carol Loomis, *Fortune Magazine*—chose one-third of the questions. The rest came from shareholders and analysts. Shareholders had e-mailed over two thousand questions to the journalists, who then selected a set of questions relating to Berkshire and its operations. The journalists, who were seated on the stage, alternated with analysts Gregg Warren (Morningstar), Jonathan Brandt (Ruane, Cunniff & Goldfarb) and Jay Gelb (Barclays Capital), and with shareholders in the audience in asking the questions.

Notations
Warren: Warren Buffett, Chairman and CEO of Berkshire Hathaway Inc.
Charlie: Charlie Munger, Vice Chairman of Berkshire Hathaway Inc.
Matt: Matt Rose, CEO of BNSF
Greg: Greg Abel, CEO of Berkshire Hathaway Energy
BNSF: Burlington Northern Santa Fe

Warren: Good morning. Before we start, two very special guests have to stand up. Even though he was on a tour, he took a quick detour. My friend Paul Anka, please stand up [applause from audience]. With all the talk about my succession, I wanted to hook up with someone famous for a possible second career. We're available for weddings, bar mitzvahs and funerals. We were offered $1,000 for Paul and me, which seemed ridiculous. I was insulted; they said OK, and offered $10,000 for just Paul. We have one other very special guest. This affair doesn't happen by itself. She even had a baby boy named Brady in September. She organized everything here today; please thank Carrie Sova [applause].

OK, now we get to the minor players and will introduce the Board of Directors. We'll have the shareholders' meeting after the Q&A. We'll recess for fifteen minutes, then at 3:45 p.m. begin the shareholders' meeting. I'll introduce the board, but please hold your applause until I'm finished introducing them, then you can go crazy. In alphabetical order: Howard Buffett [President of Buffett Farms], Steve Burke [CEO of NBCUniversal], Susan Decker [former President of Yahoo! Inc.], Bill Gates [Co-Chair of the Bill and Melinda Gates Foundation], David Gottesman [Senior Managing Director of First Manhattan Company], Charlotte Guyman [former Chairman of the Board of Directors of UM Medicine], Don Keough [Chairman of Allen and Company Inc.], Charlie Munger [Vice Chairman of Berkshire], Tom Murphy [former Chairman of the Board and CEO of

Capital Cities/ABC], Ron Olson [Partner of the law firm of Munger, Tolles & Olson LLP], Walter Scott [Chairman of Level 3 Communications], Meryl Witmer [Managing member of the General Partner of Eagle Capital Partners L.P.]. That is the Board of Directors of Berkshire [applause].

We have a couple of slides then we'll move into questions until noon, back at 1 p.m., continue until 3:30 p.m. We released our earnings yesterday [Friday, May 2, 2014]. We try to do that on a Friday so you have a full weekend to digest the 10-Q [Form 10-Q is used for quarterly reports under Section 13 or 15(d) of the Securities Exchange Act of 1934] which we make available. Don't just look at the summary; it makes great reading. This is our summary slide for Q1 [1st quarter; slide shown on projector]: operating earnings were down a bit year on year, mainly accountable from our insurance underwriting business. On a quarterly basis, this segment is not very meaningful, often it is foreign exchange–related. We have $77 billion of float in our insurance business now that is ours to invest. It is underwriting profit if it doesn't cost us to hold; satisfactory in Q1 but down from Q1 last year. It is a liability on the balance sheet, but it is cost-free, it does as much good as net worth does on the balance sheet. If we average no underwriting profit over the life of the business, I'll be very happy and you should be, too. We advise you to pay no attention to quarterly or annual realized gains in securities. We make no attempt to time sales in any quarter. We focus on gains over the longer term, but ignore it in shorter-term earnings.

With that I would like to give you a preview of a vote that was taken. It is remarkable. We had a shareholder resolution to pay a dividend, implying we weren't paying any dividends because we were living in this grand style to which we're accustomed, and shareholders were living bereft of millions. We have no proxy vote service companies; we just counted the votes as they came in. Among class A, it was 90:1 against a dividend, but you may think that I stuffed ballot box, which I did [laughter]. So I took out my votes and it was 40:1 among untainted shareholders. But maybe you're thinking it is Warren and his rich friends and all the plutocrats in the class A shares who voted against it? But class B shareholders (and we may have one million shareholders of class B), remarkably, voted against paying of dividends by a ratio of 45:1. And we were not making any calls to get their vote. I'm not sure any company in the world would get quite that vote. And one more slide, which is the disturbing part of that vote: among B shareholders, 97% voted for me [to continue as CEO of Berkshire]. It's a close vote for either getting rid of me or paying dividends. The number of people who wanted to have a dividend and wanted me to get out of the place were neck and neck. So you can see why I'm averse to proposing the dividend to the Board of Directors.

Questions and Answers: Part 1

Q1. Carol Loomis from *Fortune*: We received hundreds if not thousands of questions. If we don't get to your question, please excuse us. We haven't shared with Warren or Charlie, but they read the news so some of the questions may be familiar. The first one is from Will Eldridge of New York City: Why did you not vote against the Coke compensation plan when you said it was excessive? Rather you abstained from voting, which is un-Buffett-like.

Warren: We didn't want to vote against the compensation plan because David Winters'[2] calculations about the potential dilution were highly flawed. We didn't want to get involved in that kind of accusation.

I spoke to Coke CEO Muhtar Kent privately, and told him we would abstain because we thought the plan was excessive. We announced that shortly after the vote. It is having an effect on compensation plans.

This was the most effective way to make a clear statement. We had no desire to go to war with Coca-Cola. I don't think going to war is a very good idea and if you ally with someone you have to be very sure of whom you go with. I received some letters on it, after they had been released to the press. I think it

---
[2] David J. Winters, Wintergreen Advisors, LLC.

is best to be careful of alliances with someone you don't know. I think we got the best result for Coca-Cola. Charlie?

Charlie: I think you handled it very well.

Warren: Well, then, Charlie remains vice chairman. I should point out, in fairness to David Winters, he took figures from the proxy statement, so I can't fault him for that. But for those of you who like to think about dilution, Coca-Cola has regularly repurchased shares issued, so share count has come down a bit. It involves 500 million shares, issued over four years. I'll make it simpler, and leave out options versus performance shares. That is a lot of shares. Assuming all options are issued at $40, and when exercised, the stock is $60, then this is a $10 billion transfer of value ($20×500 million shares). However, the company gets a tax deduction for $10 billion expense. At the present tax rate, this is worth about $3.5 billion in less tax. The company gets $20 billion of proceeds, add $3.5 billion of tax savings, and Coca-Cola receives $23.5 billion. Coca-Cola will likely buy back 391,666,666 shares at $60, so, in effect, the company would be out 108 million shares which, on 44.4 billion total shares outstanding, amounts to 2.5% dilution. You can change the purchase price but that doesn't change things very much. I don't like dilution, and I don't like 2.5%, but it's much less than the numbers quoted.

I think the best result for the Coca-Cola was achieved by our abstention, and we'll see what happens in terms of compensation between now and the next meeting of Coke.

Q2. Jonathan Brandt from Ruane, Cunniff & Goldfarb: Should Berkshire adopt 3G's more hands-on management approach [in place of Berkshire's hands-off management style]?

Warren: The two systems don't blend very well because of the difference in management styles. But we would very likely partner with 3G if we see more opportunities. But it is unlikely to blend the two systems. We want to remain more hands-off.

Managers, when they join Berkshire, are joining a large business unlike anything else. It is a huge corporate asset we have and it will continue to grow. We want to send a clear message to our managers. Berkshire's corporate culture is super important. It will last even when I am gone. We don't like to overstaff in our home office.

Charlie: I don't think we ever had a policy of rewarding overstaffing[3].

Warren: At least not at head office where we only feel happy when people are sitting in each other's laps. We don't wish to enforce a strong discipline on whether a subsidiary has a few too many people. It

---

[3] Berkshire employees totaled 340,499 at the yearend of 2014, up 9,754 from 2013 with no addition at headquarters in Omaha, where only 25 people work.

won't always be true. We encourage by example but not by edict.

Charlie: I think a lot of great businesses spill a little, because they don't want to be fanatics and that's OK. I don't think you have to strip every single nickel out of the cost structure. It can create a less pleasant work environment.

Q3. Station 1, Colorado: Wynn [Stephen Wynn, CEO of Wynn Resorts] said Obama is the biggest wet blanket to the economy. Since other countries are lowering taxes, can you get Obama to change?

Warren: I think I'll let you communicate with him directly.

I don't agree with a number of things you say. American business is doing exceptionally well. We'll have a difference of opinion on politics, and you won't convince me and I won't convince you. Just look at corporate profits, and a chart of corporate taxes as a percentage of GDP. Corporate taxes are down from 4% to 2% of GDP, when other taxes have increased. American earnings on net tangible assets, the measure of profitability overall, is the envy of the world. We have extraordinary returns. Our tax rate for corporates is lower now than when Charlie and I were operating. We'll call a truce. I'll let Charlie comment.

Charlie: I'm going to avoid this one.

Warren: And people complain about me abstaining.

Q4. Becky Quick from CNBC: You said "management not doing better than the index is not doing a good job." How come you didn't tackle the issue that you underperformed the index over the last five years? Are you changing the yardstick?

Warren: We're not changing yardsticks. We said in the 2012 annual report that we would do worse in very strong years and better in weak years compared to the S&P 500. I had warned in the 2012 letter that if the market did well in 2013 we would most likely break our streak of outperforming over every five-year period. Over any cycle we'll overperform. But there is no guarantee.

Charlie: Indices do not pay taxes. Warren is paying 35% taxes on his net worth. So it is a very high bar to clear. If this is failure, I want more of it.

Q5. Jay Gelb from Barclays: Since there is a difference between the market price and the intrinsic value of Berkshire, how are you going to unlock value? Would you consider an IPO of the operating units?

Warren: No, with respect to IPOs. Almost no other company discusses intrinsic value as much as Berkshire.

GEICO carries $1 billion of assets that are worth $10 billion intrinsic value. We have some other businesses with some million dollars of assets that are worth some $2 billion.

Charlie and I could get within 5% of each other estimating Berkshire's intrinsic value, but probably not within 1% of each other—intrinsic value is inherently uncertain. We like to repurchase our stocks at a discounted price compared to the intrinsic value. We think 1.2 times book value is a bargain for Berkshire shares: that's why we're willing to repurchase shares at up to that level.

Charlie: We've never wanted Berkshire stocks to be overvalued so that we can issue it to others. It is OK for it to be a bit lower than intrinsic value. We're not in the game to balloon the stock price. In the long run, our stock will do better.

Warren: We've watched this in the past: conglomerates issuing stock at high prices to take over companies. It works, but if you cheat on earnings, where do you stop? That is a game we don't want to play. It is very distasteful. And it comes in waves. We don't want to come close to playing it. Unless I'm careful, Charlie will name names ... so we better move on.

Q6. Station 2, Los Angeles: Berkshire is known to buy and hold businesses for many years. But early in your career that wasn't the case. Since any acquisition can be disruptive, what did you do to gain the trust of owners?

Warren: We keep our promises. And we're careful to make only promises we can keep. We cannot promise that we won't lay people off. But we promise that we will not sell our businesses. We end up holding on to some businesses that haven't lived up to expectations.

You will not pass a course in business school if you put down our principles for why we keep some businesses, but we made a promise.

If we don't keep our promise, word would get around. We list the economic principles so managers who sell to us know they can count on it. We can't make some promises and we don't promise never to sell. But we've only had to get rid of a few businesses, including the original textile business. We also let managers continue to run their business. We're now in a class that is hard to compete with. A private equity firm won't be impressed by what we put in the back of our annual report. People who are rich and run a company their grandfather started—they don't want to hand it over to a couple of MBAs who want to show their stuff. As long as we behave properly, we'll maintain that asset, and many will have trouble competing with it. It is how we want to operate. I think it will continue to work well.

Charlie: Obviously, we behave the way we do because we like our style. Number two, it has done pretty well, that's why we're unlikely to stop [pause].

Warren: You can tell Charlie doesn't get paid by the word.

Q7. Andrew Ross Sorkin. Your son Howard Buffett is on Coca-Cola's board and voted for the compensation plan. Given Howard's role in Coke, how can we depend on him to keep Berkshire's culture intact?

Warren: I think an organization is part business and part social. I've been on corporate boards for fifty-five years; nineteen companies outside of Berkshire. I don't think I've ever seen a compensation committee vote down a compensation proposal.

The so-called independent directors on boards are typically receiving $200,000 per year or more for six days work in pleasant company: they are not independent. Boards do not look for Dobermans; they want Cocker Spaniels with their tails wagging.

Social dynamics are important in the board culture at Berkshire. Howard is the perfect guy to carry out Berkshire's unique culture. As a non-executive chairman, his role will be to facilitate a change of CEO in the very unlikely case that one is needed.

Charlie: Warren was voted down at Salomon Brothers [a Wall Street investment bank, founded in by three Salomon brothers – Arthur, Herbert and Percy with Ben Levy in 1910; now part of Citigroup]. The idea of yelling disapproval all the time is not right. In life, you have to pick your spots. If we all shout, we won't be able to hear each other.

If you keep belching at the dinner table you will soon be eating in the kitchen.

Warren: People need to pick their spots or they will not only be ignored, but also not be heard on other issues. Charlie gives the marital advice around here: attempting to change the behavior of others.

Charlie: I offend more people than you do, and I am satisfied with the level of disapproval.

Q8. Gregg Warren from Morningstar: Regarding management performance, what do you think the firm's cost of capital is? Is it changing as the firm grows?

Warren: There's no question that size is an anchor to performance. With a $300 billion market cap, we cannot earn the returns on capital we had in the past.

Our cost of capital is the return that could be produced by our second-best idea. Our best idea has to exceed that.

If we put some billion dollars in one business that is worth more in present value terms than what we've invested, we'll keep them.

We try to produce more than $1 of value for every $1 we spend—we focus on opportunity cost. We recently bought Altalink, an Alberta electricity transmission company for $3.2 billion, and we'll be better off and that was the best thing to do that day with that $3 billion. I've never seen a CEO wanting to do a deal and a CFO say it didn't exceed the cost of capital.

I've heard lots of nonsensical explanations about cost of capital. No one really knows what their cost of capital is.

Charlie: Cost of capital means different things to different people and often means silly things to people who work in business schools. Warren's definition of adding more in market value than we put in will never be taught in business school. The phrase "to retain to create more value," is the best description. It's simple: we're right and they're wrong.

We just don't focus on cost of capital. We consider our options, and try to pick the one that will deliver the best returns.

Warren: I look good compared to him, don't I?

Q9. Station 9, Omaha [Audience question]: How were you able to buy Nebraska Furniture Mart so cheaply? What were the economic conditions in Omaha back then?

Warren: We paid a price. It was not a bargain price: we paid slightly more than book value. We paid eleven or twelve times earnings. It had $100 million sales, pretax 7% margin, or about 4.5% after tax. It was a great business, but not a bargain. It was a fair price for a wonderful business and a great opportunity to get involved with a great family.

On my birthday in 1983, in August, I gave a letter to Mrs. B [Mrs. Rose Blumkin, who founded Nebraska Furniture Mart in 1937], and Louis [Louis Blumkin, Chairman Emeritus of Nebraska Furniture Mart and son of founder Rose Blumkin]. Her son told her what was in it. I asked, did she owe any money and did she own the building? "No" and "Yes, she did." If you want to talk bargain purchases, we should talk about going out to Nebraska Furniture Mart for shopping. We had a record $40 million in sales for the week last year. We're up 7% now vs. last year. On Tuesday we did $7.8 million.

I was in Dallas last week. We're opening the Nebraska Furniture Mart of Texas. The 1.3 million square foot distribution center and the 560,000 square foot retail showroom will become the largest home furnishings store in North America when it opens in spring 2015.

Q10. Carol Loomis: In your will you said to put 10% in short-term bonds and 90% in a low-cost S&P 500 index fund. Why did you suggest an index fund instead of Berkshire shares?

Warren: When I die, every single share I own will be distributed to five foundations over the course of ten years. My views on Berkshire are so solid that I can't think of any better way to do it. For my wife, it is not a matter of maximizing capital; it is about maximizing safety and not doing worse. It is about peace of mind. On the part I care about maximizing, I've instructed the trustees not to sell any of the Berkshire shares until they have to.

Charlie: Warren has a peculiar way of donating his money and he has every right.

Warren: Do I hear any of my children applauding?

Charlie: You are down to a few trifles. Warren (Susie was the same) really is a meritocrat. He wants money to go back to civilization in which it was earned. I like being associated with it.

Q11. Jonathan Brandt: BNSF has done well, but Union Pacific [a railroad franchise that operates 8,000 locomotives over 32,000 route-miles covering 23 states across the western two-thirds of the United States] seems to be doing better. What service challenges is BNSF facing? And what are the differences between the two railroad companies that may lead to divergent results?

Warren: We've handled more volume than in the past. In 2006, we did 219,000 peak carloads. We've had a lot of service problems on the Northern Route. We've been spending more money than Union Pacific to anticipate problems in terms of future demand. And when you get a big increase in volume on that one route, from Bakken shale oil, there are a lot of trains running now that weren't running five years ago. Harsh winter weather has created a lot of service disruptions for BNSF. I'll let Matt [Rose] address some of the cold-weather problems.

Matt: Industry grew at over 100,000 units and we handled 53% of the units. Oil came a lot faster than we expected. We've been spending to build into it. I've been CEO for thirteen years, and I've never seen weather like this past winter. We had eighty-three inches of snow in Chicago. There were many days with below-zero temperatures in Minnesota. We handled 206,000 units last week. No railroad has handled 205,000 units. Our volumes are largely determined by our geography. We're doing everything we can to handle the volumes.

Warren: We'll spend $5 billion on the railroad this year. I received calls from North Dakota. They were complaining about fertilizer. I assured them fertilizer would be there on time. We did fifty-two [cars], and they will get there in time for the planting. We take it seriously. BNSF earnings will do a lot better next year.

Q12. Station 4, Omaha: In the future, how do you ensure an adequate supply of natural gas? What do you do when gas prices rise?

Warren: We're the largest generator of alternative energy in the country. By 2015, we'll meet 40% of our demand from alternative energy. It is unlike any other company you can find in the country. Greg [Abel] will answer specifics on natural gas dependent units. I'm not worried about the issue you raised; we have the opportunity to shift to coal.

Greg: Matt touched on the very cold winter we had in the Midwest. We were challenged. We need natural gas to get heat and lights on. This past year we were in renewables: 39% of energy produced in Iowa was renewable energy. We're cost-effective and well positioned to serve our customers better. However, we have a very flexible system. We can alternate between generation sources depending on market conditions.

Warren: 8% of the natural gas that we use in Omaha is supplied through a pipeline that we own. We purchased a natural gas pipeline from Enron (and

Dynergy in-between). The pipeline had the worst reliability in the industry at the time of purchase due to underinvestment, and now it is the most reliable.

Q13. Becky Quick: Has there been any discussion about who, if anyone, will replace Charlie Munger?

Warren: Whoever replaces me as CEO will likely choose someone he will work with very closely. It's good to operate with a partner.

Charlie is my canary in the coal mine. Charlie just turned 90. I'm encouraged by how he's handling middle age.

But now I'm getting sensitive—you raised a point—they talk about replacing me, but they never talk about replacing Charlie. Berkshire is better off with two of us working together.

I do think Coca-Cola's Goizueta and Keough or Capital Cities' Tom Murphy and Dan Burke accomplished far more because of two incredible people with complementary talents.[4] It is a great way to operate. You can't will it to somebody. I'd be very surprised if a few years after a successor takes over, there wasn't some relationship or partnership. It can enhance achievements and the fun they have. But no one has brought up a successor to Charlie.

---

[4] To learn more about great partnerships, see *Working Together: Why Great Partnerships Succeed* by Michael D. Eisner (HarperBusiness).

Charlie: I don't think the world is concerned about a 90-year-old guy who is gone.

Warren: The canary has spoken.

Q14. Jay Gelb: Who can replace Ajit Jain? What does Matt's move to chairman at BNSF mean for Berkshire?

Warren: You can't replace Ajit. Only a reincarnation of Ajit Jain would be able to replace Ajit. We'll not have another Ajit to replace him.

The BNSF move is not related to Berkshire as a whole [Matt's role was shifted to that of executive chairman of BNSF in December 2013, renewing speculation he might be in line to replace Warren Buffett]. I have every manager send me a letter with their views of who should replace them if someone is incapacitated. In some they talk about more than one person, and strengths and weaknesses. I wouldn't make assumptions about subsidiaries.

Charlie: I am not the least bit worried about it. I wish my biggest problem were succession at Berkshire. I think we're in a good situation.

Q15. Station 5, Minnesota: If you had to invest your entire net worth in one company in 2009, what would that be?

Warren: Great question, but it is not going to get an answer.

Charlie: I think you gave the right answer.

Q16. Andrew Ross Sorkin: Would you be willing to show the compensation for some more top executives? How much should the next Berkshire CEO be paid?

Warren: We follow the SEC rules [Executive Compensation and Related-Party Disclosure Rules, 2006] in terms of whose pay gets disclosed.

Berkshire's next CEO should be entitled to get a lot of compensation; how much he or she accepts is a different question.

The new CEO will deserve to be paid a lot, and we'll talk about it more in next year's letter.

Shareholders won't be better off by publishing more people's salaries. If you do that, people might want more when they see what everyone else makes. It is seldom that publishing compensation accomplishes much for the shareholders. At Salomon Brothers, everyone was satisfied with their salaries, but they felt worse when they came to know the salaries of others.

When management made secret deals with the arbitrage group whereby Meriwether [John Meriwether, former vice chairman and head of bond trading at Salomon Brothers] got paid a lot of money (and I would argue they earned it), the jealousy that broke out was a problem.

I think CEOs would be getting paid a lot less if everyone else's pay wasn't disclosed in proxy statements.

Charlie: In a spirit of transparency, you are asking for something that wouldn't be good for shareholders. So we aren't going to do it. We're better off by not adding to the culture of envy in America. Our practices are envy dampeners.

Warren: No CEO looks at someone else's proxy statement and comes away thinking they should be paid less.

Charlie: Envy is doing this country a lot of harm.

Q17. Gregg Warren: Should Berkshire use some of its cash to extinguish its debt? And why let the energy group keep all of their cash, but BNSF has to pay a dividend back to the parent?

Warren: BNSF is not going to buy another business. BNSF generates plenty of earnings and can handle increased debt, so it distributes excess earnings to Berkshire. Berkshire Hathaway Energy [formerly Mid-American Energy] should have a lot more acquisition opportunities, so it retains its earnings. We spent a substantial amount on NV Energy [provides electricity to 2.4 million customers in Nevada with a service area covering 44,000 square miles, acquired by Berkshire in 2013], and we just bought transmission lines in Alberta. At BNSF, we'll spend a lot of money to have the best railroad possible, but we won't buy other businesses at BNSF.

At Berkshire Hathaway Energy we need money from shareholders. 90% is owned by Berkshire, and Greg [Abel] and Walter Scott, Jr. [Director of Berkshire Hathaway Inc.] have the balance. If we need more equity we'll have a pro-rata subscription. They may opt out but purchases will improve the value of their shares. We may invest billions there.

We'll always keep $20 billion cash on hand for liquidity. We don't count on the kindness of others. Berkshire doesn't count on bank lines or anything else. We lent to Harley-Davidson at 15%. Harley-Davidson is a fine company, but they needed cash [Berkshire bought $300 million of Harley-Davidson's long-term debt nearly six years ago]. When you need cash, it's the only thing you need. Available cash is like oxygen: you don't notice it 99% of the time, until it's absent.

Charlie: We're very lucky to have the businesses. Now we're so affluent. It's a blessing to have capital-intensive businesses like BNSF and Berkshire Hathaway Energy, which give us an opportunity to reinvest large sums of capital at attractive rates of return.

Warren: Compound interest will catch up with us. It has dampened things, but not delivered its final blow yet.

Q18. Station 6: How do you handle capital allocation and your relationship with Munger?

Warren: When we first met, I was twenty-nine and he was 35. We disagreed on a lot of things, but Charlie and I've never had an argument in over fifty years. We argue with others.

Charlie: Most of the time we think alike. That is a problem; if one of us misses it, the other is also likely to.

Warren: The really big mistakes have all been my fault. I'm more inclined to action than Charlie is. Would you say that's right, Charlie?

Charlie: You once called me the "abominable no-man."

Warren: Back to the first part of the question, the cash from the subsidiaries. We don't count the money in the energy business or railroad. It doesn't matter where the money sits, so we aren't worried about how much cash subsidiaries should send to the parent. I know where the cash is. I can get it when I need it. Maybe a sweep account would make sense. We're not big disciplinarians. Berkshire is flexible in terms of where to park the money, whether it's at the holding company or at the operating subsidiaries.

Charlie: And that's just fine.

Q19. Carol Loomis: In an interview in April, you said I hope we get questions on our weak points. What are Berkshire's weak points and what can be done to address them?

Warren: We have a lot of weak points, and I try to point them out. Maybe we should be more disciplined about taking back cash from the operating subsidiaries. We could possibly be earning a slightly higher return than it is. We're very disciplined in some ways but very sloppy in other normal business matters.

A clear weak point is that I'm slow to make personnel changes. I love the managers we have, but sometimes I don't act fast enough to replace someone when it needs to be done.

Charlie: I don't know exactly. Sweep account system, it's like a friend who went to give blood and it wasn't flowing very easily and they started squeezing his arm.

Warren: Our managers are listening—don't give them that metaphor.

Charlie: I don't like the idea of every dollar that comes in that it gets swept away. Teledyne [an American industrial conglomerate, founded in 1960 by Henry Singleton and George Kozmetsky] and Litton [an American defense contractor, founded in 1953 by Charles Litton, Jr.], swept every dime every day, and it created a tone in the company that is less desirable. We took one manager from an executive chair to an Alzheimer's home.

Warren: That is sensitive subject, Charlie.

Charlie: I want to be careful.

Warren: We operate differently in terms of supervision and we don't have a general counsel at Berkshire. There will be times when our lack of supervision of subsidiaries will mean we miss chances for improvement. On the other hand, if we managed them more closely we would miss out on lots of positives that we wouldn't have thought of. On balance, we think Berkshire is better off by giving the operating subsidiaries free rein.

Charlie: By the standards of the rest of the world, we over-trust. But our results have been much better than the rest of the world. We've selected people that we can trust. Places work better when they create a culture of deserved trust. I think tightly measured internal controls will do more harm than good.

Q20. Jonathan Brandt: See's [an American candy manufacturer, founded by Charles See, his wife, Florence, and his mother, Mary, in Los Angeles in 1921] is one of your favorite businesses. Profit growth has stalled since 1999. What has changed? Did you consider a geographic expansion?

Warren: The business of boxed chocolates has not been growing much. Boxed chocolates have lost position to salty snacks. If you go back a hundred years, the size of any city is characterized by the size of chocolate shops. Predecessor to Pepsi-Cola was a candy shop; most stores were in New York City.

Charlie: Charles Guth [an American businessman and an executive of Loft Candy who purchased the trademark and syrup recipe from the twice-bankrupt Pepsi-Cola].

Warren: See's has done remarkably well versus other chocolate companies. We can't do much about increasing the size of the market. We've tried moving out of a strong geography multiple times. What we were earning in California in 1970s was great, but we tried to move national and we didn't get rich. It doesn't travel that well.

Charlie: Sometimes it does and sometimes it doesn't. You find out what works by trying it.

Warren: In the East they prefer dark chocolate, in the West it is milk chocolate. We've tried lots of things, but See's can't overcome a stagnant market. See's hasn't done well in new geographies—the brand usually doesn't travel.

But See's continues to provide lots of earnings that we've reinvested elsewhere. More importantly, See's opened my eyes to the power of brands. We've made a lot of money in Coca-Cola, partly thanks to See's. If we hadn't acquired See's in 1972, we wouldn't have seen the value in Coke in 1988.

Charlie: The main contribution to Berkshire was "ignorance removal." Berkshire would have been nothing if we hadn't bought See's. We were pretty damn stupid when we bought See's— just a little less stupid enough to buy it. The best thing about Berkshire is that we've removed a lot of ignorance. The nice thing is we still have a lot of ignorance to remove.

Warren: That's what happens when I call on Charlie.

Q21. Station 7: Why did you make the shift in the Bank of America investment?

Warren: Brian [Moynihan] of Bank of America called me and asked if we would be willing to change preferred stock from cumulative to noncumulative so that it could be counted as Tier 1 capital, improving Bank of America's regulatory capital ratios.

Ben Graham identified noncumulative preferred stock as a terribly weak form of securities in the *Security Analysis*.[5] But Brian asked whether we would be willing to make our preferred non-callable for five years. In a world of 5 basis-point money, I was very willing to make that trade-off. I get five-year non-callable 6% preferreds, which I can use as payment for the warrants we have.

That provides a nice return in a low-yield world. The probability that going to noncumulative will hurt us was very small. The probability of not being able to reinvest the money at a comparable return was much higher.

Charlie: Well, I agree with you.

Q22. Becky Quick: What are the current prospects for NetJets [a subsidiary of Berkshire Hathaway that offers fractional ownership and rental of private business jets]?

Warren: NetJets is a perfectly decent business. But we need more unit volume. NetJets' business is correlated with the economy and the performance of the stock market in 2007-2008. A fair number of people who are our customers are fund managers who didn't renew their membership during 2011-2012.

---

[5] *Security Analysis*, 6th Edition, by Benjamin Graham and David Dodd, (McGraw-Hill; Foreword by Warren Buffett).

In the last six months, the net ownership is down. NetJets is not a huge growth business any more, but nobody is remotely close to us. At the same time, we don't see that the market will double or triple very soon.

The European market is also declining. Berkshire is bringing NetJets to China soon, but it's a very long-range play. The good news is flight hours have picked up; that means flight owners are using their hours.

Charlie: I demonstrated my confidence by buying twenty-five more hours.

Warren: It was a tough sale.

Q23. Jay Gelb: Would IBM, American Express, or Wells Fargo ever be used as a financing source for large-scale acquisitions?

Warren: Not likely. They could be a source of funds but we are unlikely to sell them. Berkshire is about building earnings power. We're always looking for opportunities to add to our earnings power. If an attractive-enough opportunity came along, we would be willing to sell stock holdings. This could happen this year or ten years from now, you never know.

Charlie: No, I think we have businesses such as BNSF and Berkshire Hathaway Energy that will generate enough cash to invest in other companies.

Warren: What we really want is to buy whole businesses. But we're in no hurry to sell our stocks. If we did need to raise funds by selling stocks, they wouldn't be the ones you mentioned.

Q24. Station 8, Italy: How about increasing leverage in Berkshire? Why don't you issue several billion dollars of bonds with long maturities and make good use of it?

Warren: What you say makes great sense. But if you had asked us forty years ago, given our current mix of businesses and current interest rates, we would have probably been willing to take on more debt.

Charlie: It wouldn't have been a hard decision.

Warren: We have a way to generate cash through our insurance float of $77 billion. We don't like the idea of operating in a conservatively leveraged environment and adding a lot of leverage.

We have no problem with adding leverage to the utility and the railroad. We have a better way of generating funds than others. Using equity for BNSF made the deal happen, but it wasn't necessarily a good idea.

Another $30 or $40 billion of debt at Berkshire wouldn't be a problem, but we don't want to change course now, especially since we have other attractive sources of funds (like float).

We don't have many places to put all this money. If an attractive $50 billion deal came along, we would find a way to do it.

Charlie: Even though your suggestion is intelligent, we will not do that.

Q25. Andrew Ross Sorkin: You have investments in things like renewable energy and electric cars like BYD [a Chinese automobile manufacturer based in Shenzhen], but BNSF carries lots of coal. What are the risks and opportunities posed by climate change?

Warren: It can have an impact on our insurance business. If we own railroads, that's a lot of coal. BNSF will carry less coal at some point in the future.

When Ajit and I talk about catastrophe insurance, we talk about the probability of a hurricane in Florida or earthquake in New Zealand. The impact of climate change on year-to-year catastrophe probabilities is very low. We'll continue to develop alternative forms of energy. We're happy to carry the coal.

We're a common carrier by law, so even if we wanted to turn down coal we could not. We don't think climate change should be a factor in making investment decisions.

Charlie: I think that most who claim climate change will change tornadoes and storms, are mostly overclaiming. There is clearly global warming. But people who claim to know exactly what is going to happen are talking through their hats. We're agnostic.

We're going to need a lot more electricity made from wind and sun. Berkshire is positioned well with investments in renewable energy generation and transmission lines.

We're beautifully positioned but don't deserve credit for it, we just stumbled into it.

Q26. Gregg Warren: Ted [Weschler] and Todd [Combs] now manage much more money. But they still manage less than $7 billion of all equity positions. How much money does each of them run now? And how much do you want that to grow?

Warren: Ted and Todd are managing little over $7 billion now. We'll change that upwards, but not month by month. They will be handling more money in the future. Things get difficult as the size gets larger. It is better to move money to them and away from me as time passes.

They are both terrific for Berkshire. Each knows a whole lot of our businesses and culture. They don't ask for extra compensation. They are 100% attuned to Berkshire. It's been a big, big plus for us. They will be more important as years go by.

Charlie: Nothing there.

Q27. Station 9, Toronto: Are low rates leading to a housing bubble or potentially a bond bubble? If you were running the Fed [Federal Reserve System], what would you do or suggest?

Warren: Who would have guessed [interest] rates would be this low for this long? I would say I am surprised at how well things are going. It is working well. I don't think I'll do things differently. I'll do the same thing and take credit. It is a very interesting move; we haven't seen it before and we don't know how it will end.

I think Ben Bernanke [Chairman of the Federal Reserve from 2006 to 2014] was a hero both at the time of the crash and subsequently. He is a very smart man. I looked at the 2007-2008 Fed meeting minutes, even the members did not know what's going on. He was not getting unanimous support from those around him. But he went ahead with them, and did a masterful job.

Charlie: Nobody, for example, in Japan, anticipated that interest rates would stay down for twenty years and common stocks would decline for twenty years.

Strange things have happened, and it is confusing to economists. If you aren't confused, probably you don't understand the problem very well.

Warren: People cling to cash at the wrong times. The current policy has not created a bubble. It is just unusual. Zero interest rates have tremendous effect on the economy. This is not a bubble situation we're living in, but it is unusual.

Charlie: I am not as confused as you are.

Warren: That's why we get along so well.

Q28. Carol Loomis: You've been looking for bear, but that's silly. I'm not a bear on Berkshire. But conglomerates rarely work well, but it has for you so far. What is the probability that it will work for your successor?

Warren: Business did well in the U.S. over time. Look at Dow Jones as a changing group of companies over a hundred-year period. Seeing the index rise from 66 to 11,000 suggests it is a good model, although, admittedly, it is not all under one management team. Owning a good number of businesses is not a terrible idea. Litton Industries, Gulf & Western [an American conglomerate, founded in 1934] and LTV [Ling-Temco-Vought, an American conglomerate, founded in 1947, filed for Chapter 11 bankruptcy on December 29, 2000] were put together on the idea of serial acquisitions by issuing stock at 20×earnings to buy businesses at 10×earnings. It is an idea of fooling people to ride on a chain-letter scheme.

I think our business plan works. We own a diversified group of very high quality, well managed, conservatively capitalized companies. The idea of capitalism is to allocate capital. And we can allocate capital from one area to other more promising areas (say, from See's Candies to other businesses without any tax consequences). No one is better positioned than Berkshire to do that. Lots of the conglomerates of the past have been primarily focused on stock promotion, *not* business-like promotion.

Charlie: There are a couple of differences between us and the failures in the conglomerate model. We have an alternative when there are no companies to buy; we have more insurance businesses. We have no compulsion to buy businesses. Mellon brothers [Andrew W. Mellon and Richard B. Mellon, American bankers, industrialists, and philanthropists] did well for 50–60 years. They are a lot like us. We're not a standard conglomerate like Gulf & Western. We're as if Mellon brothers had gone on forever.

Warren: Now you're talking.

Q29. Jonathan Brandt: Why is Forest River [an American manufacturer of RVs, pontoon boats, cargo trailers and commercial vehicles] doing so well? Is Forest River taking lower margins to beat Thor [an American manufacturer of recreational vehicles]? With three companies with 85% of the market, it is harder to have a new competitor enter.

Warren: Peter [Peter Liegl, CEO of Forest River, founded the company in 1996] is not an MBA-type person. He built a successful RV business and sold it to private equity, which subsequently ran it into the ground. The CEO then repurchased the company out of bankruptcy and rebuilt it. This time he sold it to Berkshire, which hasn't meddled in the operations.

We went to dinner that night and he brought his wife and daughter, made a few promises, and we've lived happily ever after. I've never been to the factory in Elkhart, Indiana. I've had three or four phone calls with him the whole time. We made a deal on incentive compensation and base compensation. It will do over $4 billion of revenue this year.

It's a tough business, but the CEO is exceptional and he knows what he's doing. It's a business with 11–12% gross profit margin with a 5–6% SG&A [Selling, General & Administrative Expense].

But it works for him and it's worked for us, as well. We could use twenty more companies like his. Like GEICO, it is also the leader in the industry.

Q30. Station 10, Toronto: What is your view of oil sands and its impact on Berkshire?

Warren: In terms of oil sands, it is not a huge impact on Berkshire. We have a crane business in Marmon that is active in the oil sands. They will soon have a transmission operation of eight thousand miles that will cover most of Alberta.

We own some ExxonMobil and they have oil sands. We're moving seven thousand barrels of crude oil per day on our railroad. We have nine unit trains that carry a hundred cars, and each car has 650 barrels. There is significant advantage to take it to different places; spreads are different. Mentally you think of oil gushing through pipelines, but the pipeline is twice as fast. We recently bought Phillips Specialty Products Inc., a unit from Phillips 66, that provides flow-improver products to customers worldwide. I think the oil sands are an important asset for mankind over the coming decades, but I don't see a dramatic impact on Berkshire.

Charlie: A lot of oil sands' production uses natural gas as an input. So it's only good business if oil prices are high relative to natural gas prices.

Matt: Nothing to add.

Warren: An update on the S&P 500 vs. fund of funds bet.

[Puts up a slide of performance from 2008–2013 of hedge fund performance]. The cumulative return between 2008 and 2013 is 43.8% for S&P index fund and 12.5% for the hedge funds.

Six years ago I made a bet for charity[6]. It was an S&P 500 Index fund versus a group of hedge funds. With those numbers, the comparison is getting more fun every year. The people who selected these funds are smart people. They have every economic incentive to pick the best. They choose from at least two hundred hedge funds whose managers are also incentivized to enhance their own income. The first year they did considerably better, but in five years subsequently the S&P 500 has been running away. We put in $350,000 each into ten-year treasuries. The way interest rates changed we sold the bonds at 96 and put it all in Berkshire stock, and I guaranteed it for $1 million. It will be significantly more than $1 million when ten years comes along.

We'll be back in an hour and move on from there.

… Recess …

---

[6] Buffett vs. Protégé Partners, LLC
http://longbets.org/362/#adjudication_terms

"When we know that a company we own but don't control is going to make an acquisition, I'm more likely to cry than smile." Warren Buffett

"Competence is a relative concept. I realized that what I needed to do is compete against idiots, and luckily there is a large supply." Charlie Munger

Questions and Answers: Part 2

Warren: If you can find your seats, we'll get started. I'll give you another minute or two to settle down.

We sent out about eleven thousand more tickets this year, and clearly this year we have substantially more attendants than in years past and I hope spending patterns reflect that!

Q31. Becky Quick: After the Energy Future Holdings bankruptcy [formerly TXU Corp., filed for Chapter 11 bankruptcy protection on April 29, 2014], what regulations or technological changes do you think could affect Berkshire's business?

Warren: Energy Future Holdings was a mistake on my part. We do make mistakes and we'll make some mistakes in the future. In the case of Energy Future Holdings, I had a fairly simple assumption that gas prices would go up in the future, but gas prices went down. Just like Energy Future Holdings, I was caught off guard by a changing market.

All our businesses are subject to change, not subject to huge changes. For example, GEICO originally achieved low costs by direct mail marketing to government employees. They've had to adapt with the technology over the years: telephone, Internet, now social media. They expanded beyond government employees as well.

I'll make mistakes in the future. In the past we made some mistakes, too: the department store in Baltimore that we bought in 1966. There was nothing dumber. The $6 million in that store became $45 billion over time in Berkshire. You have to be very alert, and Charlie and I and our directors think about it.

Charlie: I spoke earlier about the desirability of removal of ignorance, piece by piece. Another trick is scrambling out of your mistakes. It is enormously useful. We had a sure-to-fail department store, a trading stamp business sure-to-fold, and a textile mill. Out of that came Berkshire. Think about how we would have done if we had a better start.

Warren: My great-grandfather started a grocery business in 1869 in Omaha. Later my grandfather operated the grocery store before it closed in 1969.

We know our businesses won't look the same in five or ten years. Our subsidiaries generally see more gradual change and are starting from a position of strength. We also look for managers who are on the lookout for change and able to adapt.

Q32. Jay Gelb: Talking about Heinz [an American food processing company, founded by Henry Heinz in 1888, acquired by 3G Capital and Berkshire in 2013] acquisition, what do you expect Heinz's earnings to be when they file their earnings?

Warren: Heinz will publish their own 10-Q. Heinz has historically been a typical, steady food business with 15% operating margins. They invited me to have a look at the earnings quarter-by-quarter. I think their earnings will improve quarter-by-quarter.

Because of the brand and cost structure, I expect profitability to improve substantially under new management.

Q33. Station 11, Philadelphia: How do you think about comparing investment opportunities? Would Berkshire have done better concentrating on a few of its favorite companies like Coca-Cola and American Express rather than investing in so many different areas, especially during the 2008–2009 panic?

Warren: I spent a considerable amount of cash during 2008–2009 crash and the bottom was quite a bit lower than September and October of 2008. We were also committed to $16 billion of Mars [one of the world's leading food manufacturers known for its chocolates and candy, as well as pet care, food, and drink products] funding. We didn't do remotely as well as if we had kept the powder dry and spent it all at once at bottom.

Our timing could have been better in 2008–2009. We started buying too early. Timing could have been improved dramatically, but we'll never be able to figure out how to do it. But we bought BNSF in October 2009, which will be an enormous part of our future. When we bought Home Depot bonds at fifteen we should have bought the stock, but that will always be the case. What we want to do at our present size and scope—we're interested in big businesses with the right management.

We want to be able to add them without issuing shares. Looking back, we can do it better than we have done it. I feel the game is still a viable one, but it can't be forever. But it still has juice left in it.

Charlie: Private businesses are becoming bigger in Berkshire. We have big portfolios of common stock. But our private businesses will be more than our common stock portfolio.

Warren: When we're right about stocks, it shows up on market value. But if we're right about companies, it shows up on future earnings power.

Charlie: You can't judge your performance compared to what could have been achieved by buying stocks at the absolute bottom. First of all, you can never tell where the bottom is except in retrospect. Second, you probably wouldn't have been able to buy a significant volume of shares at those low prices.

Warren: There is a trade-off between risk and return. If copper prices go up, you will make the most money in the lowest-quality copper producer, because they have the highest marginal cost and the most earnings leverage. But that doesn't mean the low-quality company offers an attractive risk/reward trade-off before the fact.

Charlie: We've adapted and the changes have been very much in our interest. There may be future changes just as desirable. Since change is inevitable, how you adapt to it is the key.

Warren: We've bought a fair amount of Wells Fargo over the last few years. But the most money was made by buying banks of lesser quality. During 2008–2009, we were 100% comfortable buying Wells Fargo and 50% comfortable buying others. So we went where we were most comfortable.

Q34. Andrew Ross Sorkin: How will usage-based pricing affect GEICO's performance? Google is trying a self-driving car. Would you sell GEICO?

Warren: No. If you know the customer's information before you sell insurance, that helps to determine the proper premium. Insurance companies can use propensity of a particular driver in an accident as a variable in determining the proper premium. We think we have a good system for evaluating risk, and it has worked very well historically. Progressive [an insurance company] has done a lot of work on it. It's called Snapshot®[7]. Insurance is about evaluating the probability of loss in order to establish the proper premium.

If someone is ninety, besides Charlie, of course, they are more likely to die. There are variables in insurance, and a set price. If you live in state of one million rather than 100 million, there's a lot less chance of accident, due to lack of density. Through studying usage by various methods, Progressive is trying to get better information about the probability of that particular driver getting in an accident.

I feel very, very good about GEICO and their ability to evaluate risk. I don't think anyone is better than GEICO's people. If self-driving cars work and substantially reduce accidents, it will be very good for society and very bad for auto insurers like GEICO. I just don't know. We won't sell GEICO no matter what, though.

Charlie: Surprisingly, things happen very slowly and the impact is unlikely to be meaningful. I went to a speech about thirty years ago, about color movies coming into a house on demand—that it was just around the corner. I think self-driving cars having huge impact on market will take some time. That would be my guess, but it could be wrong.

---

[7] A system for monitoring people's driving habit, http://www.progressive.com/auto/snapshot/

Warren: Then we'll be wrong together!

GEICO will be doing more business in five years and ten years from now and in thirty years. I'll go away peacefully and you'll know and I won't.

Q35. Gregg Warren: Berkshire deployed very little capital outside the US except ISCAR. Why?

Warren: We've never turned down an opportunity abroad just because it is abroad. We just haven't had as much luck as getting on the radar screen of owners outside the U.S.

We tried to make significant acquisition. Recently we made this Alberta deal. We like to buy from the founder of the businesses. Almost all founders/family owners who want to sell their business in the U.S. are aware of Berkshire, and many prefer to sell to Berkshire. Foreign companies don't approach Berkshire nearly as much.

Stef Wertheimer [a German-born Israeli business magnate, philanthropist, politician and founder of ISCAR Metalworking Companies (IMC)] wrote us a letter, and said if they didn't sell to us they wouldn't sell. I've been a little disappointed we haven't had more luck. They sell tiny little cutting tools that go into basic industry all over the world. They buy them because they are using them up. In March and April they are seeing strength in business, so it is hard to see that this means weakness in the industrial world. ISCAR has been wonderful; wish I could find a few more like it. This year we've not been contacted by any significant ones that made sense. We've heard from people but nothing that makes sense.

Q36. Station 1, San Francisco: How does someone figure out one's circle of competence?

Warren: You need to be self-realistic in appraising your abilities and knowledge. Charlie and I are reasonably good at that. In my own case, I am good at retail. Retail is easy to understand. When we purchased Berkshire, it was out of my circle of competence.

Lots of CEOs don't know where their circle of competence begins and ends. But we have a number of very good managers who understand that. All of them are like Mrs. B. Mrs. B doesn't understand stocks, but cash and real estate. So when we acquired Nebraska Furniture Mart, she wanted cash.

Ask your friends, probably they might help.

Charlie: I don't think it is difficult to figure out competence. If you are 5'2", you have no chances for the NBA; or if you are ninety-five years old, you don't have many more years left; or if you weigh 350 pounds, you don't dance lead in the Bolshoi ballet [founded in 1776, a renowned classical ballet company at the Bolshoi Theatre in Moscow, Russia]. If you can't count cards, don't compete in poker.

Warren: You are ruling out everything I want to do!

Charlie: Competence is a relative concept. I realized that what I needed to do is compete against idiots, and luckily there is a large supply.

Q37. Carol Loomis: Why do you compare the performance of the S&P to Berkshire's growth in book value per share? It is not rational at all; it seems like apples and oranges, since Berkshire is primarily an operating business these days.

Charlie: I'll answer this one. The answer is you are totally right. It makes no sense and it makes it difficult for Warren to look good. But he likes to set hard challenges. It's ridiculous and insane, but it is right.

Warren: Normally I like to clarify when he goes all wishy-washy but I won't this time.

Q38. Jonathan Brandt: Multiples paid for recent acquisitions were higher than historical purchases—why? In case of Marmon and ISCAR, why did you change the valuation formula?

Warren: The multiples that we used for ISCAR is from the 2006 original transaction: multiples of earnings and allowed for cash. ISCAR had a put option and we had a call option, to govern between now and judgment day. There was no variation in the formula. Put and call at the same price, following the same formula. They put it to us exactly on the same basis.

But Marmon transaction was an installment sale, a different type of deal. We intended 60% but did 64%. We looked at consequences of formula in future. They wouldn't have sold the first piece if they didn't have the second and third. We knew we would be paying more money later on, but it was all built into the original deal.

Charlie: If the value of the businesses went up, then the price will go up as well and we pay for value.

Warren: Both Pritzker [one of the wealthiest families in the United States, owns Hyatt hotel chain and Marmon Group] and Wertheimer [one of the richest families in Israel, founded ISCAR] families behave better. Feelings are good on both sides.

Charlie: We have enormous respect for intelligence in these two families [both Pritzker and Wertheimer]. Absolutely amazing what they have done.

Warren: Those were two important acquisitions, partly due to accounting peculiarities, where carried value is much lower than the intrinsic value.

Charlie: The tanker business in Marmon is John D. Rockefeller's original business. It's amazing how businesses can keep their value.

Warren: Life circles back around, you may meet people you think are one-stop shops but they aren't.

Q39. Station 2, New Jersey: If you were a twenty-three-year-old, which non-tech industry will you go into and why?

Warren: I would do the same thing I did when I was twenty-three: I would go into the investment business. I would see CEOs of eight or ten coal companies. I would ask them, if they had to put all of their money into any coal company except their own, and go away for ten years, which one would it be? And which would they sell short over ten years, and why? If I did that, I would know more about the coal companies than any manager would. But you wouldn't learn about how to start Google or Facebook that way. You need real curiosity about it, it has to turn you on. Asking questions about coal companies? I mean, really, you have to be a little odd, too. I might find an industry that particularly interested you, and you might become very well equipped, and you can start or go to work for someone good in that industry. If you are open to things and keep learning things, you'll find something.

Charlie: There was a trick Larry Bird [retired American professional basketball player] used. He asked every agent why he should be selected to represent him, and which agent to use if Larry didn't pick him as his agent. Everyone listed the same guy as number two, so he went with everyone's number two, and he negotiated the best deal in history.

Warren: I did the same thing at Salomon. On the weekend when Tokyo was opening Sunday at six p.m., I called in eight people and I asked them who besides you would be the best person to run Salomon. One guy said no one but him. I eliminated him right away. But it is not a bad system to use. I think you can learn a lot about the team this way.

I sound like a Yogi Berra[8] quote, perhaps. But if you talk to enough people about something they know a lot about, people like to talk... Here we're talking ourselves. You will find your spot. I was very lucky, I found what fascinated me when I was seven or eight years old. If you are lucky you will find it early.

Charlie: If you obviously don't have a talent for something, it's OK to give up on it and move on to something else. When I went to Caltech, there was a course on thermodynamics. I immediately decided I wasn't going to be a thermodynamics professor at Caltech and moved on. I did that with field after field, until pretty soon there was only one or two left.

Warren: I had a similar experience in athletics.

---

[8] Former Major League Baseball catcher, manager, and coach, who is known for his witty quotes.

Q40. Becky Quick: You complained about price-gouging by hotels, etc. during the Berkshire weekend in Omaha. Isn't this just supply and demand?

Warren: Yes it is, which is why we've encouraged Airbnb[9] to come to Omaha.

A big industry has to go to Las Vegas or a place with lots of rooms. If you have an event which can't be sized by people scheduling it, you can outstrip the rational supply of rooms. The Masters Golf tournament in Augusta has this problem as the tournament won't move any place else. Omaha can't size to the Berkshire meeting; our attendance has grown above what we anticipated.

The three-day minimum booking bothers me a lot. Hilton Omaha didn't do that. We didn't want to move to Dallas. Omaha people love this event and people get a good impression of Omaha. And we want hotels to make money. This is an economic boom for them. Airbnb is a flexible supply arrangement, and seems to make a lot of sense. I hope they will do better next year.

Charlie: I have nothing to add.

---

[9] A community marketplace for people to list, discover, and book unique accommodations around the world.

Q41. Jay Gelb: About GEICO, will the auto insurer eventually surpass State Farm in terms of market share?

Warren: No one knows the answer. GEICO has 10% market share vs. State Farm's 19%.

State Farm is a terrific company. The company was started by farmers in Merna, Illinois, with no insurance experience. State Farm is really strong in homeowners' insurance with satisfied customers.

Allstate was long the number two. It took years for GEICO to displace Allstate as the second-largest insurer.

GEICO came up with a very good business model. I'll tell GEICO that I'll do my part. Tony Nicely [CEO of GEICO] is doing a nice job. Before Tony, GEICO market share was 2% [fifteen years ago]. Since he took over in 1993, we've gained market share so we now have 10%. It will keep growing.

I believe GEICO will have the number one position by the time I reach my 100th birthday [seventeen years from now].

Charlie: GEICO to me is very much like Costco. Very few companies have a great product at a great price. Those that do tend to steadily gain market share over time.

Warren: What is true about Costco is also true about GEICO. People (employees) come to us and don't leave us. We have very few managers from other insurance companies. They have their own idea about how to do it and do it right. It is reinforced by success, too.

Charlie: Costco is unbelievable. It's against the human nature of many entrepreneurial people to get price down and get service up, like wearing the ultimate hair shirt. But it works.

Q42: Station 3, Chicago: How has your frugality helped Berkshire Hathaway shareholders?

Warren: Who is more frugal, Charlie or me?

Charlie: In personal matters, Warren is more frugal.

Warren: Would you care to give examples?

Charlie: Warren has lived in the same house since the 1950s.

Warren: I moved in in 1958.

Charlie: I moved in a year later and paid the architect $1,900; 30% of the regular price.

Warren: I have everything in life I wanted. I don't believe standard of living is linked with cost of living. There is a point where you get an inverse correlation.

My life would not be any different if I had six or eight houses.

Charlie: Frugality has helped Berkshire. I look out at the audience, and I see frugal, understated people. We collect these people.

Warren: But forget about that this weekend: the more you spend the more you save.

Q43: Andrew Ross Sorkin: Pfizer is buying AstraZeneca to move the headquarters and reduce taxes. Would Berkshire do something similar?

Warren: No. What do you say, Charlie?

Charlie: Not a good idea.

Warren: We could not have done this anywhere but the U.S.

Charlie: I can't see Berkshire being as prosperous as it is and not paying our share of taxes.

Warren: That doesn't mean we voluntarily pay more taxes than we have to. We follow the rules and we pay taxes. We take advantage of tax incentives when they're available. But we've made lots of money over the years and paid lots of taxes.

Q44. Gregg Warren: How attractive does BNSF find the Mexican market?

Warren: Union Pacific's rail network is much better positioned for Mexico than BNSF. It crosses the border in six places. We know Kansas City Southern [a transportation holding company that has railroad investments in the U.S., Mexico and Panama] has operations in Mexico. But it doesn't make sense for us to be in Mexico. But we continue to think about Mexico and some other places.

Charlie: It's awfully easier to dream than to realize something. But with our size, we wouldn't get approval to buy competitors. I'm afraid BNSF will have to get ahead on its own.

Warren: And it will.

Q45. Station 4, Los Angeles: About intrinsic value again, and which company you fear the most as a threat to Berkshire?

Warren: Actually Ben Graham wasn't too specific about intrinsic value in terms of calculations. It may be private business value, which is the present value of predictable future earnings. Aesop invented the concept of intrinsic value: "A bird in the hand is worth two in the bush."

The question is: how sure are you that two are in the bush, how far away is the bush, what are the interest rates? Aesop wanted to leave us something to play with over the next two thousand years so he didn't spell it all out. In calculating it, Ben would say he wanted two dollars of cash in the bush and pay a dollar.

Phil Fisher[10] depends on qualitative factors to estimate the number of birds in the bush. I started out very influenced by Graham, so more quantitative, then Charlie came along and said we should look more at qualitative factors. If you buy a McDonalds' franchise, you think about the cash in, the cash out, when, and at what discount.

Silver-bullet question: are there any threats?

I don't see any big competitor to Berkshire. Private equity is buying businesses and leverage is cheap; so they are competing with us. That is the main occupation for me and Charlie. I don't see anyone who has a model or is trying to build a model which is going after what we're trying to achieve.

Charlie: The Berkshire model as it is now constructed, as they say in show business, has legs and will go a long time. It is credible. Very few big, successful companies stay that way. We're in territory where many stop going well, but I think we'll be like Standard Oil [established in 1870, it was an oil producing, transporting, refining, and marketing

---

[10] An American stock investor and author of the 1958 investment classic, *Common Stocks and Uncommon Profits* (Wiley)

company in the U.S.]. You young people in the audience: don't be too quick to sell your stock.

Warren: Why not more copycats?

Charlie: It's like our friend Ed Davis [an Omaha doctor and Buffett and Munger family friend, who introduced Buffett to Munger in a restaurant in Omaha in 1959], the surgeon. He figured out how to do an operation with instruments of his own creation, and the death rate was 2% vs. others whose were 20%. Surgeons came to watch and they said, well, that looks too hard to do and it is slow. There is nothing in business school that teaches people to do what we do at Berkshire.

Warren: Slowness deters more people.

Charlie: The difficulty with being slow is you're dead before it's finished.

Warren: Why so cheerful?

Q46. Carol Loomis: I have more on the cheerful side. This question is about inflation. Should investors be thinking more about inflation? How will that affect Berkshire if we have higher inflation in the future?

Warren: Of course, higher inflation in the future will hurt us and many more businesses. Berkshire's earnings would be up, its intrinsic value would be up, unless we leveraged the businesses, but value per share in real terms would go down.

Charlie: In Weimar Republic [federal republic and semi-presidential representative democratic government, established in 1919 in Germany to replace the imperial form of government], people who owned companies like Berkshire would survive, though. Banks and life insurance were all wiped out. But it is not a good thing to let things go that far. It's better to have subpar growth, but it would be crazy to let politicians print more money.

Warren: But if you have a home and the mortgage goes down in value, you still have the home.

Charlie: In Weimar, they gave you the mortgage back. They got that right.

Q47. Jonathan Brandt: How do you benchmark your acquisitions?

Charlie: Sum total of all acquisitions done by U.S. corporations has been lousy. It is the nature of successful companies that they will be talked into dumb deals. We're a lot peculiar and nobody wants to be like us.

Warren: When we know that a company we own but don't control is going to make an acquisition, I'm more likely to cry than smile. If you take your eyes off the ball and push towards a deal, you will make a bad deal. We're eager to do deals that make sense.

Charlie: Some are mediocre.

Warren: Look at GEICO: it had been an incredible business until the 1970s. They made acquisitions after getting back on track and then took their eyes off the ball. Accounting cost of those acquisitions was poor but not disastrous. But secondary effects were huge. It was a dozen years there that they couldn't get back. We bought half the company, so it was wonderful for Berkshire. It is human nature. CEOs have animal spirits and supporting staff senses that they like to do things. They keep coming in with deals. Investment bankers are calling them daily. All these forces push towards deals. We've tried very hard to not be eager to do deals; just to be eager to do deals that make sense. That would be harder if we had strategy departments pushing us. The setting in which you operate can be very important.

Charlie: Note how he is much more tactful than me.

Warren: The comparison is not difficult.

Q48. Station 5, Wisconsin: Do you believe financial crisis will come back? Is criminal activity on Wall Street being institutionalized?

Warren: Charlie, you are a lawyer.

Charlie: I think behavior on Wall Street has been improved due to trauma. But you are never going to have perfect behavior when humans live in miasma of easy money.

Warren: What about prosecuting individuals instead of corporations?

Charlie: I do think a few prosecutions would help shape/change behavior. If you put eagle scouts in jail after fixing steel prices, you really get behavior change.

Warren: I lean towards prosecuting individuals. At Salomon, I saw bad acts by only a few people, and negligence by a couple more without thinking about thousands of employees. It is much easier for a prosecutor to win a case against a company vs. an individual because the company is anxious to settle. They will cave and write a check. It is a tougher job against individuals since they are trying to stay out of jail.

Charlie: That is what I meant. When antitrust is considered a venal sin, it changed behavior. We changed individual behavior in price fixing. We probably need some more in finance to change behavior.

Warren: We have 300,000 people working in Berkshire. I don't know who is doing what. Someone may be doing something wrong. To a degree it is out of our hands. I can tell managers that reputation means more than anything else.[11] But it doesn't cure everything. We want to find it out early and it is up to

---

[11] Warren reiterated the same in a memo sent out to all Berkshire Hathaway managers ("The All-Stars") on December 19, 2014

us to do something about it. We'll have a problem. Three hundred thousand people will not behave properly every day. Individual prosecution helps. The way to change behavior is to have the fear that it will come home to them and hit them hard. If the only fear is that the company will write a big check, there will be much less change than if you target individuals.

Q49. Becky Quick: Is it a good idea to set up a public fund to compensate someone injured in a train accident?

Warren: We're on both sides of this. There is a federal authority to oversee the movement of hazardous materials. The major railroads carrying hazardous materials can buy insurance from Ajit. Ajit is willing to write a very high-limit policy to any railroad, but so far they haven't liked his prices.

Companies don't like to discuss how much insurance coverage they carry because it can turn into a honeypot. Nuclear risk is huge and government doesn't allow us to insure that risk. I don't think any major accident by private industry could be larger than they could pay, but it could be very large.

Charlie: British Petroleum was a big surprise. BP's Deepwater Horizon disaster was a huge cost from one failed well. No one thought loss from one well would be many billions of dollars. After that I would have less enthusiasm for drilling in the Gulf. The biggest rail accident cost $200 million.

Warren: Norfolk Southern [a railroad company operates 20,000 route miles in 22 states and D.C. in the U.S.] never announced what it cost. We do not get paid enough to carry chlorine and they will move somehow. But that doesn't keep me awake at nights.

The biggest risk is from a rogue state, terrorist act or cyberattack. War acts are excluded from insurance. But you could have a terrorist act that would create damages like we've never seen. There is a reasonable probability of this happening in the next fifty years.

Charlie: We saw what one pilot can do [Malaysia Airlines flight MH370, en route from Kuala Lumpur to Beijing disappeared with 239 people onboard on March 8, 2014]. We're lucky that we live in a world that has many big companies that can handle loss when it occurs.

Q50. Jay Gelb: Why is Berkshire Specialty Insurance expanding into commercial property and casualty lines, and why now, when pricing has peaked?

Warren: We entered commercial insurance in the middle of last year. We think we have the expertise and reputation to be successful in commercial insurance. We have a great amount of capital and ability to underwrite most intelligently. Our cost is below the industry average.

We can put the elements together and get Ajit to oversee the operations. We entered it because we had terrific people. We were not looking at the timing. We'll build a significant commercial insurance business over time and are likely to operate with better results than the competitors.

Charlie: It is logical for us to do. When it is logical we don't hold back because of the place in the cycle. Pricing may turn better soon, and it's a long-term play.

Warren: When we see a business with the right people, we'll tag along.

Q51. Station 6, Chicago: Would you buy a professional sports team?

Charlie: Warren has already done it.

Warren: I own 25% of a local minor league team, but it is not responsible for my position on the Forbes 400. If you hear us talking about buying a sports team, it's time to start talking about successors.

Sports equipment is not a good business. We own Spalding and Russell Athletic. Generally speaking, it is not a particularly profitable business. It is hard to be in the sports equipment space because Berkshire would be a target for lawsuits. Charlie, are you looking at the Clippers?

Q52. Andrew Ross Sorkin: What do you think of the rise of activist investors?

Warren: I don't think it will go away and it scared the hell out of management. In general, I don't think they are looking for a permanent position.

There are cases where corporate managers should be changed. Once the activists get the price of stock up, that will end their interest in the business—they are not looking for permanent changes in the business. It is attracting more and more money. Funds are flowing to these activists, so they can play on a bigger scale. If successful, it will create fund flow until it is no longer successful.

Charlie: Activists make a lot of money and people don't care how you make money. So that makes it grow, like Jack and the beanstalk [an English fairytale]. You'll find an activist who you don't want to marry into your family; it is like fox hunting: "the unspeakable in full pursuit of the uneatable" [*A Woman of No Importance* by Oscar Wilde, an Irish writer and poet, remembered for his novel, *The Picture of Dorian Gray*]. I don't think activists are good for America.

Warren: What do you think will happen to activist investors three years from now?

Charlie: It will be a lot bigger.

Warren: Wow, then it will be really serious, especially if you think about compounding.

Q53. Gregg Warren: If size is an issue, does it make sense to look at a bunch of smaller, faster-growing businesses?

Warren: We would be delighted to buy companies with $2–3 billion. A subsidiary could buy something for a couple of hundred million. We're not passing up on anything of any size that will have real impact. We had twenty-five bolt-on acquisitions last year. One $30 billion transaction is equivalent to ten $3 billion deals. We're working to build earning power into Berkshire, so our main emphasis is on bigger deals.

Charlie: I agree with that. Hundreds of small businesses? It would be anathema.

Warren: There is lots of competition in small deals—private equity is all after them. We aren't envious. It is not going to be the future of Berkshire.

Q54. Station 7, San Francisco: What is the most intelligent question you've been asked recently?

Warren: No good answer to that. Charlie, I'll let you handle this first.

Charlie: Someone asked me whether there is a lot of irrationality to compare Berkshire's book value per share with S&P 500.

Warren: Best question in the past?

Charlie: I don't like the question, do you? I don't think it is fair.

Warren: That's why I let you go first. We're at fifty-four questions, so I'll move to Station 8.

Q55. Station 8, New Hampshire: Looking at page 64 segment data for the energy business, when I take **EBITDA** less **CAPEX**, the result is negative operating cash flow. When I repeat the exercise in each of last five years, in the best years, $300 million of operating cash flow. Divide by tangible assets, 0.8% return. My question is, why are we investing in utilities when they don't deliver free cash flow?

Warren: You were doing great until return on tangible assets. We love the math you describe, as long as we get return on capital investment. But we'll keep investing. At some point, no investment will be required.

We did a lot better than most utilities because we're cost-effective and our rates are significantly below our competitors'. We have a good reputation with the regulators. They are going to treat us fairly. If you can put up more money, we'll generate a fair return. I think if you calculate "net cash generated" you will get a better perspective.

We have a similar situation in BNSF.

Charlie: If the numbers are coming from retail, we should be worried, but in case of utilities we're fine with the numbers.

Warren: Greg [Abel], can you quote some rates?

Greg: We're low-cost producers in our region, or at least in the lowest quartile, and we have supportive regulators. We avoid rate increases by operating very efficiently. We recently had our first rate increase in Iowa in sixteen years and we don't anticipate another in the near future.

We try to keep our capital spending close to depreciation. The major share of our capital expenditures is growth capital.

Warren: Tech companies?

Greg: We service Google, with a relatively small data center, in Council Bluffs. We supply them with very low rates and a significant portion comes from renewable energy. We're also building a 1,000-megawatt electricity facility in Iowa.

Q56. Station 9, Shanghai: How do you see the U.S. and Chinese educational markets changing in the future?

Charlie: We certainly are getting the easy questions!

Warren: Whatever he says, I agree with.

Charlie: I think America made a huge mistake to allow the public school system to go to hell. I think Asian cultures are less likely to do that. China is trying not to repeat our mistake. I wish we were more like them.

Warren: It reminds me whenever I get a little worried about Charlie…[pause]… Maybe, I shouldn't talk about that. There is a joke about not hearing well that goes like this. I asked the doctor, "Look, Doc, I got this partner of mine. He is losing his hearing. Would you let me know what can I do?"

After the doctor's visit I stood at the opposite side of a room and asked in a normal speaking voice, "Charlie, do you think we ought to buy GM at $35?" No response.

So I moved to the middle of the room and asked again: "Charlie, do you think we ought to buy GM at $35?" Again, no response.

So I moved right next to Charlie and asked one last time: "Charlie, do you think we ought to buy GM at $35?"

Charlie responded: "For the third time, yes!" So speak up.

Q57. Station 10, Chicago: Do we need housing finance reform in Freddie Mae and Fannie Mac? Would Berkshire get into this business?

Warren: The thirty-year, fixed-rate mortgage is a boon to homeowners. There is not enough private capacity to insure all of these mortgages, so the government needs to be involved. But that makes it political. You cannot keep the politics out of this. And then Fannie Mae and Freddie Mac did stupid things by themselves.

Berkshire is unlikely to participate in this market, because other people would be more optimistic than them in setting premiums. In the end, the government needs to be the main insurer.

Charlie: Well, private industry will take over. There are idiots and thugs. I hate politicians as much as you do. Freddie and Fannie are conservative today, and they're issuing most of the mortgages. I think that's OK.

Warren: The one thing that led Fannie and Freddie astray was serving two masters trying to deliver double-digit earnings increases. It would have been fine if they just insured rather than buying portfolios and turning themselves into big hedge funds, and just borrowed cheap and lent long.

Charlie: I think they are being conservative now.

Warren: And portfolio activity?

Charlie: I think it is a mistake to have private companies taking over the whole mortgage market. There is no need to have private portfolios. I think that particular experiment in privatization was a total failure.

Warren: I was not going to mention it.

Q58. Station 10, Whitney Tilson: There is a new book on 3G Capital [*Dream Big* by Cristiane Correa] but only in Portuguese. What's the secret sauce for 3G Capital? Why do they enjoy a better deal? And a long-term personal relationship with 3G seems to be really important; will a successor be able to do this?

Charlie: Why would you assume shareholders don't read Portuguese?

Whitney: The only English print copies in the world are here. On Amazon it is a Kindle book.

Warren: We'll raise the price.

Whitney: Is there a Berkshire stamp of approval on their deals? What will happen to the value of the Buffett brand to buy companies?

Warren: Our Brazilian friends are very smart, focused, determined, hard-working and never satisfied. They don't overreach or overpromise. We're very fortunate to associate with them. My successor will act very similar to me in making deals (that's part of the Berkshire brand).

Charlie: The way to get a good spouse is to deserve a good one. It is the same with partners. You deserve a good partner if you just behave as one yourself.

Warren: What can we learn from 3G?

Charlie: 3G is removing unnecessary costs, and I don't think there's anything wrong with that. It should be done with sensitivity, but I think it's good for society.

Warren: And sensitivity.

Charlie: But our system should not have make-work.

Warren: We're learning from them.

Charlie: Everyone is, some reluctantly.

Q59. Station 11, Taiwan: I named my first son after you, Warren. What will Berkshire look like in twenty years?

Warren: How is he doing?

Q59: He is only four. He calls you "Warren Buffaloes."

Warren: I've been called worse.

Q60. Station 1: What will Berkshire look like in twenty years?

Warren: I do plan on writing about that next year. No question we'll have more cash than we can intelligently deploy in business. That will depend on circumstances at the time. If stock can be bought in that makes sense for continuing shareholders, that creates better value for them, I would be aggressive. We'll have more cash than we can intelligently invest in the future. I hope it isn't real soon but I don't think it is on the distant horizon. The numbers are getting to that point but maybe we can repurchase shares. But what is done will be done in the interest of shareholders. We don't know what taxes will be, but every decision will be made in the principal interest of the shareholder.

Charlie: It is not a tragedy to succeed so much that future returns go down.

Q61. Station 2: What implications will the sharing economy (for example, Uber, Airbnb) have on those sectors?

Warren: Whenever an existing business is threatened, that business will fight back. When GEICO first came around, most insurance was sold through agents. The incumbent insurance companies tried to fight back, in part through state laws restricting how insurance could be sold. In the end, the one with the better mousetrap usually wins.

We stay away from businesses that we know will change and we do not know who the winners will be. Our energy company and railroad are both very likely to be winners over time. Where change is involved in other fields, we sit and watch but don't get tempted.

Charlie: New technology can be quite disruptive to a lot of people. I think retail is facing some very significant threats from new technology. I think Berkshire by and large is in good shape.

Warren: Where are we most vulnerable?

Charlie: I don't want to name those here.

Warren: Now you have them wondering.

Q62. Station 3, Florida: What's the best way to promote financial literacy? Do you think financial literacy should be part of the school curriculum?

Warren: The earlier the better. Habit is such a powerful force in everyone's life.

I am very sympathetic about your point. We want to talk to people at a very young age. There is a big problem with adult financial illiteracy. Anything you can do very early through the school system would be good.

Schools are your best bet. Lots can be done using the Internet. For children, we have "Secret Millionaire Club[12]." There is an exhibit in the hall.

Charlie: I am not sure the schools are responsive. I would place most of the blame with the parents.

Warren: Many people don't have the right parents. How would you fix them?

Charlie: It is very hard to fix people with wrong parents. It gets so impractical. I don't think I'm good at that. The only thing I'm good at is raising the top higher. The main problems in education are probably not in the grade schools. There is a lot of asininity at universities, in the economics departments. When it gets more complicated it doesn't mean it gets a lot better.

Warren: There was a period of twenty years when the net utility of finance majors' knowledge was negative.

Charlie: It was asinine. We should use normal English.

Warren: I watched extraordinary universities teach people very dumb things. To obtain positions in departments in those schools you had to subscribe to the orthodoxy. But that may have soured my feeling

---

[12] An animated series that features Warren Buffett as a mentor to a group of entrepreneurial kids, http://www.smckids.com

on higher education, and it was bad. Was my language OK?

Charlie: You would have liked academics better if you had taken physics rather than finance.

Q63. Station 4, Ontario: Is there a logical way to break up Berkshire into four large companies?

Warren: We'd lose significant value if we broke Berkshire into four companies, because of capital allocation and tax reasons, among other things. Even if it is possible, we will not do that. Investors can cash out some portions of their position, if needed. There would be no advantages with breaking. That would be a terrible mistake.

Charlie: You will not be deprived when stock goes from 100 to 200 and you do not get a dividend.

Warren: Shareholders voted 45:1 against a dividend. That margin surprised me. It would be a mistake to change.

End of Q&A session

Epilogue

As aptly stated by Bill Gates that as a member of the Berkshire Hathaway board, the weekend of the AGM "is one of the most enjoyable 'duties' of my year."[13] We agree. Attending Berkshire Hathaway shareholders meeting is one of the best ways to spend a weekend. We consider Warren Buffett's letters to the shareholders and their (Warren and Charlie's) answers to the questions at the AGM as the best lessons in finance and investment.

You are probably reading this book because you see yourself (just as we see ourselves) as a student of value investing, specifically registered in the school of Warren Buffett and Charlie Munger. We hope if you attended the 2014 AGM, this book has been a refresher and you now have a record of it so that you can revisit Warren and Charlie's perspectives on the questions that were asked. If you were not able to attend the meeting, then this is your access to the Q&A session. We hope this format will continue and we will continue to learn from these legends.

We expect this year's (2105) meeting to be equally informative, enlightening, fascinating, and fun. While we have no idea what questions will be asked, we expect people to be curious about decisions such as getting out of Exxon Mobil, increasing the Berkshire stake in IBM, Warren and

---

[13] http://www.gatesnotes.com/About-Bill-Gates/Master-Class-with-Warren-Buffett-Berkshire-Hathaway-Annual-Meeting-2014

Charlie's take on the stalling of the Keystone XL pipeline project, the impact of falling oil prices, what plans they have for acquisitions in Europe, when to buy what and when to sell, and much more. Furthermore, we expect a lot interesting questions in light of both Warren and Charlie's reflection over the past fifty years and their view of the prospects for Berkshire's future (as they describe in the 2014 letter to shareholders). It is definitely worth attending and we encourage all shareholders who can to attend.

As always, we expect investment wisdom that is certainly worth keeping record of. We will do our best to take accurate notes and to present them in a reader-friendly form.

About the Authors

Eben Otuteye

Eben Otuteye is Professor of Finance at the University of New Brunswick, Fredericton, Canada. Professor Otuteye joined the Faculty of Business Administration at UNB in 1987 where he has been teaching various finance courses, including principles of finance, corporate finance, investments, value investing, personal financial planning, and theory of finance, in both the BBA and MBA programs.

Dr. Otuteye's research interests include behavioral finance, value investing, asset pricing models, portfolio management strategies, and the economics of e-business, topics on which he made many conference presentations all over the world and published in several high-ranking journals.

In collaboration with Mohammad Siddiquee, Professor Otuteye developed a heuristic (the O-S heuristic) for making value investing decisions. This is a system that incorporates the value investing principles as originally propounded by Benjamin Graham and its extensions as developed and practiced by Warren Buffett and Charlie Munger.

Mohammad Siddiquee

Mohammad Siddiquee is a Lecturer in Finance at the University of New Brunswick Saint John. He studies behavioral finance as well as the psychology of decision making in investment management.

Influenced by the works of Benjamin Graham and his disciple Warren Buffett, Mohammad is also studying value investing. He is working with Dr. Otuteye on the project "Redefining Risk," which may lead to rethinking traditional risk-return paradigms.

Mohammad teaches managerial finance, investment and portfolio management and personal financial planning in the undergraduate program, and corporate finance and entrepreneurial finance in the graduate program.

Mohammad is currently working on his doctoral studies at the University of New Brunswick. He is an avid value investor and runs a value investing web portal, http://patienceinvesting.com.

Index

1

10-Q, **16**, 57

3

3G, **21**, **86**, 87

A

academics, **91**
acquisition, **25**, **36**, 54, 57, 61, 74
AGM, **8**, **10**
AGMs, 9
Ajit Jain, **13**, 34
Allstate, 68
Altalink, 28
American, **13**, **14**, 22, **36**, 39, 41, **44**, **49**, **50**, **51**, 57, 65, 72
analysts, **14**
Andrew Ross Sorkin, **14**, 26, 35, **46**, 59, 70, 80
Annual General Meeting, **7**, **8**
annual reports, **8**

B

balance sheet, **16**
bargain, **24**, **29**
Becky Quick, **14**, 23, **33**, **43**, 55, 67, 77
behavior, **27**, 75, **76**, 77
Benjamin Graham, **7**, **43**, **95**, **97**
Berkshire, **7**, **8**, **10**, **13**, **14**, 15, **17**, **21**, 23, **24**, **25**, **26**, **30**, 33, **34**, 35, **36**, **37**, **38**, **39**, **40**, **42**, **43**, **44**, **45**, **47**, **49**, **50**, **51**, **52**, **53**, **55**, **56**, **57**, **58**, **61**, **62**, **63**, **67**, **69**, **70**, **71**, **72**, **73**, **74**, **75**, **76**, 78, **79**, **81**, **85**, **86**, **87**, **88**, **89**, **91**
Berkshire Hathaway Inc., **7**, **8**, **14**, 37
Bill Gates, **10**, **13**, **15**
BNSF, **14**, **15**, **31**, **32**, **34**, 36, 37, **44**, **45**, **46**, **58**, 71, **82**
Board of Directors, **15**, **17**
book value, **24**, **29**, **63**, **81**
British Petroleum, 77
business management, **8**
business schools, **9**, **28**
buy back, **20**

C

capital, **27**, **28**, **30**, **37**, **38**, **42**, **49**, **61**, 78, **82**, **83**, 91
Carol Loomis, **14**, **19**, **30**, **39**, **49**, **63**, 73
cash, **36**, **37**, **38**, **39**, **44**, **45**, **48**, 57, **62**, **63**, **72**, 82, 88, **91**
CEO, **14**, **15**, **17**, **19**, 22, **26**, **28**, **31**, 33, 35, **36**, **51**, 68
Charlie Munger, **7**, **8**, **7**, **8**, 9, **13**, **14**, **15**, **33**, **54**, 95
China, **44**, **84**
chocolate, **41**
Cities Services, **7**
class A, **17**
class B, **17**
CNBC, **14**, 23
Coca-Cola, **19**, **20**, **26**, **42**, 57
Coke, **19**, **21**, **26**, **42**

common stock, **58**
compensation, **19, 21, 26, 35, 47, 51**
compensation plan, **19, 26**
Competence, **54, 63**
Compound interest, **37**
conglomerate, **39, 49, 50**
corporate asset, **21**
corporate profits, **22**
corporate taxes, **22**
cost of capital, **27, 28**
Costco, **68, 69**
culture, **21, 26, 36, 40, 47**

D

David Winters, **19, 20**
debt, **36, 45**
dilution, **19, 20**
dividend, **17, 36, 91**
Dow Jones, **49**
Dynergy, **33**

E

earnings, **16, 22, 24, 29, 32, 36, 42, 44, 49, 57, 58, 59, 63, 71, 73, 85**
economics, **8, 90, 95**
education, **9, 90, 91**
Energy Future Holdings, **55**
Enron, **32**
equity firm, **25**

F

Facebook, **65**
finance, **8, 76, 85, 90, 91, 95, 97**
float, **16**
Forest River, **51**
formula, **63, 64**

Fortune Magazine, **14**
Frank Sinatra, **14**
frugal, **69, 70**

G

GDP, **22**
GEICO, **24, 52, 55, 59, 60, 61, 68, 69, 75, 88**
Goizueta, **33**
Google, **59, 65, 83**
Graham, **7, 9, 43, 71, 72**
Greg, **14, 32, 37, 83**
Greg Abel, **14**
Gregg Warren, **14, 36, 47, 61, 71, 81**

H

hands-off management, **21**
Harley-Davidson, **37**
hedge funds, **53, 85**
Heinz, **57**
hockey, **13**
holding company, **38, 71**
Home Depot, **58**
Howard Buffett, **15**

I

idiots, **54, 63, 85**
ignorance, **42, 56**
index fund, **30, 53**
insurance, **16, 45, 46, 50, 59, 60, 68, 69, 74, 77, 78, 79, 88**
interest rates, **45, 48, 53, 71**
intrinsic value, **23, 24, 64, 71, 73**
investment, **8, 7, 8, 27, 42, 46, 57, 65, 72, 82, 97**
IPO, **23**

ISCAR, **61**, **63**, **64**

J

Jay Gelb, **14**, **23**, **34**, **44**, **57**, **68**, **78**
Jonathan Brandt, **14**, **21**
journalists, **14**

K

Keough, **15**, **33**

L

leverage, **45**, **59**, **72**

M

market cap, **27**
Marmon, **52**, **63**, **64**
master class, **10**
Matt Rose, **14**
MBA, **7**, **51**, **95**
Mellon brothers, **50**
Meriwether, **35**
mortgage, **74**, **85**, **86**
Mrs. B, **29**, **62**
Muhtar Kent, **19**

N

natural gas, **32**, **52**
Nebraska Furniture Mart, **13**, **29**, **62**
NetJets, **43**, **44**
New York Times, **14**
Norfolk Southern, **78**
Nuclear risk, **77**

O

Olympics, **13**
Omaha, **7**, **8**, **13**, **29**, **32**, **56**, **67**, **73**

P

Paul Anka, **14**, **15**
Phil Fisher, **72**
pipeline, **32**, **52**
portfolio, **7**, **58**, **85**, **95**, **97**
portfolio management, **7**, **95**, **97**
Pritzker, **64**
profitability, **22**, **57**
Progressive, **60**
promise, **25**

R

railroad, **31**, **32**, **37**, **38**, **45**, **52**, **71**, **77**, **78**, **89**
renewable energy, **32**, **46**, **47**, **83**
repurchase, **24**, **88**

S

S&P 500, **23**, **30**, **53**, **81**
S&P 500 Index, **53**
safety, **30**
Salomon, **27**, **35**, **66**, **76**
Salomon Brothers, **27**, **35**
SEC, **35**
See's, **41**, **42**, **50**
shareholders, **8**, **14**, **15**, **17**, **35**, **36**, **37**, **69**, **86**, **88**
short-term bonds, **30**
Standard Oil, **72**
State Farm, **68**

stock, **7, 20, 24, 42, 43, 44, 49, 50, 53, 58, 72, 73, 80, 88, 91**
subsidiaries, **34, 38, 39, 40, 56**
subsidiary, **21, 43, 81**
succession, **15, 34**
successor, **33, 49, 86**
sweep account, **38**

T

tax, **20, 22, 29, 50, 70, 91**
Thor, 51
Tony Nicely, **68**

U

U.S., **13, 49, 61, 70, 71, 73, 74, 78, 83**
underwriting, **16**

Union Pacific, 31, 71

V

value investing, **7, 95, 97**
vote, **17, 19, 26**

W

Wall Street, **7, 8, 75**
Warren Buffett, **7, 8, 7, 8, 9, 13, 14, 34, 43, 54, 95, 97**
Weimar Republic, **74**
Wells Fargo, **44, 59**
wisdom, **7, 8, 9**
Woodstock of Capitalists, **8**

Y

yardstick, 23
Yogi Berra, **66**

www.ingramcontent.com/pod-product-compliance
Lightning Source LLC
Chambersburg PA
CBHW051730170526
45167CB00002B/881